Usborne Activities

Chocolates & Sweets to make

Rebecca Gilpin and Catherine Atkinson

Designed and illustrated by Non Taylor

Photographs by Howard Allman

Additional design by Doriana Berkovic

Contents

Beside each ingredients list, you can find out how long the chocolates and sweets will keep.
If you give them as a present, make sure you also tell the person you are giving them to.
In lots of the recipes, you will use teaspoons and tablespoons for measuring.
Use measuring spoons if you have them, as they give you exactly the amount you need.

Sweethearts

To make about 30 sweethearts, you will need:

50g (2oz) icing sugar
50g (2oz) caster sugar
100g (4oz) ground almonds*
100g (4oz) full-fat sweetened condensed milk
red food dye
one small and one very small heart-shaped cutter
a baking sheet lined with baking parchment

These sweets need to be eaten within four days.

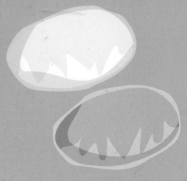

1. Sift the icing sugar into a large bowl. Add the caster sugar and ground almonds and stir them all together.

2. Make a hollow in the middle and add the condensed milk. Mix it in well, until the mixture is completely smooth.

3. Put half of the mixture into another bowl. Add two drops of red food dye. Mix in the dye really well, using your fingers.

4. Wrap both pieces of mixture in foodwrap. Put them in a fridge for 20 minutes. This makes them easier to roll out.

5. Sprinkle a little icing sugar onto a clean work surface. Roll out the pink piece, until it is about as thick as your little finger.

6. Use the larger cutter to cut out heart shapes. Cut them close together. Make the scraps into a ball, and roll it out.

2

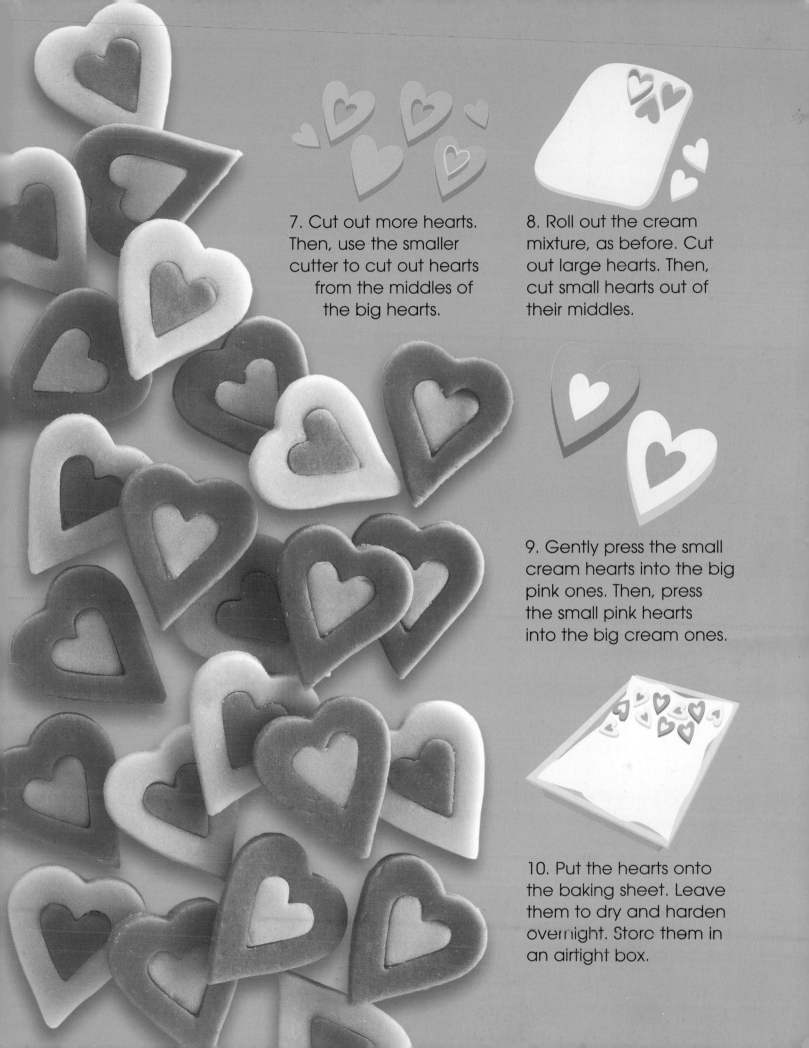

7. Cut out more hearts. Then, use the smaller cutter to cut out hearts from the middles of the big hearts.

8. Roll out the cream mixture, as before. Cut out large hearts. Then, cut small hearts out of their middles.

9. Gently press the small cream hearts into the big pink ones. Then, press the small pink hearts into the big cream ones.

10. Put the hearts onto the baking sheet. Leave them to dry and harden overnight. Store them in an airtight box.

Tropical fruit cups

To make 12 tropical fruit cups, you will need:

50g (2oz) sweetened dried pineapple
   or mango
1 tablespoon of pineapple or orange juice
100g (4oz) milk chocolate drops
100g (4oz) white chocolate drops
small foil or double thickness paper cases

*These chocolates need to be
eaten within five days.*

1. Put the pineapple or mango onto a chopping board. Using a sharp knife, carefully cut the fruit into tiny pieces.

2. Put about a quarter of the chopped fruit on one side. Put the rest into a small bowl, and add the fruit juice. Stir it well.

3. Cover the bowl with plastic foodwrap. Leave the fruit for half an hour or until it has soaked up the juice.

Do this while the fruit is soaking.

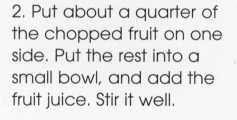

Wear oven gloves when you lift the bowl out.

4. Pour about 3cm (1in) of water into a pan. Heat the pan until the water bubbles, then remove it from the heat.

5. Put the milk chocolate drops into a heatproof bowl. Wearing oven gloves, carefully put the bowl into the pan.

6. Stir the chocolate with a wooden spoon until it has melted. Lift the bowl out of the pan. Leave it to cool for three minutes.

Spread the chocolate all the way up the sides.

7. Spread chocolate over the inside of the sweet cases with a teaspoon. Put them into a fridge for 20 minutes, until firm.

8. Spoon some of the soaked fruit into each chocolate case. Each case should be just over half full.

9. Melt the white chocolate in the same way that you melted the milk chocolate. Leave it to cool for three minutes.

10. Spoon the white chocolate over the fruit, so that it comes right to the top of the milk chocolate cases.

11. Put a piece of fruit on top of each chocolate. Chill them in a fridge for half an hour. Then, peel off the sweet cases.

12. Put the chocolates in an airtight container. Keep them in a fridge until you are ready to eat them.

Creamy coconut ice

To make 36 squares, you will need:

2 egg whites, mixed from dried egg white
(mix as directed on the packet)
450g (1lb) icing sugar, sifted
175g (6oz) desiccated coconut
4 teaspoons water
green food dye
a shallow 18cm (7in) square cake tin
greaseproof paper

Coconut ice needs to be eaten within 10 days.

1. Put the tin onto a piece of greaseproof paper. Draw around it and cut out the square, just inside the line.

2. Use a paper towel to wipe some oil onto the sides and bottom of the tin. Press in the paper square and wipe it too.

3. Put the egg whites into a large bowl. Stir them quickly with a fork for about a minute, until they are frothy.

To make pink and white coconut ice, use red food dye instead of green.

4. Stir in two tablespoons of icing sugar. Add and stir in the rest of the icing sugar, a little at a time, until it is all mixed in.

5. Add the coconut and water and mix everything well. Spoon half of the mixture into the tin. Use your fingers to press it in.

6. Add a few drops of green food dye to the rest of the mixture. Stir the mixture until it is evenly coloured.

Smooth the top with the back of a spoon.

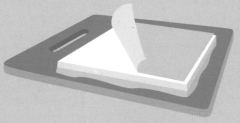

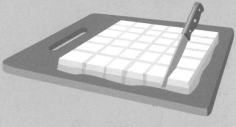

7. Spoon the green mixture on top of the white layer. Then, leave the tin in a cool place overnight.

8. Use a blunt knife to loosen the edges of the coconut ice. Turn it out onto a chopping board. Then, remove the paper.

9. Cut the coconut ice into 36 small squares. Leave them to harden for two hours. Keep them in an airtight container.

Chocolate truffles

To make about 10 truffles, you will need:

100g (4oz) milk chocolate drops
25g (1oz) butter
25g (1oz) icing sugar
50g (2oz) plain cake, crumbled into fine crumbs
4 tablespoons chocolate sugar strands
small paper cases

Chocolate truffles need to be eaten
within five days.

Put chocolate truffles in boxes
lined with tissue paper, to
give as presents.

1. Pour about 3cm (1in) of water into a pan. Heat the pan until the water bubbles, then remove it from the heat.

2. Put the chocolate drops and butter into a heatproof bowl. Wearing oven gloves, gently put the bowl into the pan.

Wear oven gloves when you lift the bowl out.

3. Stir the chocolate and butter with a wooden spoon until they have melted. Carefully lift the bowl out of the water.

4. Sift the icing sugar through a sieve into the chocolate. Add the cake crumbs and stir until everything is mixed well.

5. Leave the chocolate mixture to cool in the bowl. Then, put the chocolate sugar strands onto a plate.

Use a teaspoon.

6. When the mixture is firm and thick, scoop up some with a teaspoon and put it into the chocolate strands.

Roll the spoonful to make a ball.

7. Using your fingers, roll the spoonful around until it is covered. Then, put It In a puper case. Make lots more truffles.

8. Put the truffles onto a plate. Put them in a fridge for 30 minutes. Keep thom in an airtight container in the fridge.

Chocolate-dipped fruit

You will need:

450g (1lb) small strawberries
    with their stems left on
75g (3oz) milk chocolate drops
75g (3oz) white chocolate drops
baking parchment

The chocolate-dipped fruit needs to
be eaten on the day you make it.

You can also dip other
kinds of fruit in chocolate.
Satsuma segments look
pretty and taste delicious.

1. Put the strawberries
in a sieve. Wash them
under cold running
water for a little time,
to rinse them.

2. Gently pat them with
a paper towel to remove
most of the water. Then,
spread them out on a
plate. Leave them to dry.

3. Pour about 3cm (1in)
of water into a pan. Heat
the pan until the water
bubbles, then remove it
from the heat.

4. Put the milk chocolate
drops into a heatproof
bowl. Wearing oven
gloves, carefully put the
bowl into the pan.

5. Use a wooden spoon
to stir the chocolate until
it has melted. Using oven
gloves, carefully lift the
bowl out of the water.

6. Melt the white
chocolate drops in the
same way. Leave both
bowls of chocolate to
cool for two minutes.

7. Dip a strawberry into the melted chocolate. The chocolate should come about halfway up the strawberry.

8. Lift the strawberry out and let it drip over the bowl. Then, put it on a piece of baking parchment on a plate.

9. Dip the other strawberries into the chocolate. Then, put them in a fridge for about 20 minutes, to set.

10. Carefully peel the strawberries off the baking parchment, and put them on a plate, Eat them on the same day.

Mini florentines

To make about 18 mini florentines, you will need:

18 glacé cherries
18 unsalted halved walnuts or pecan nuts*
75g (3oz) plain chocolate drops
75g (3oz) white chocolate drops
a baking sheet lined with baking parchment

Mini florentines need to be eaten within four days.

These mini florentines are topped with pecan nuts and glacé cherries.

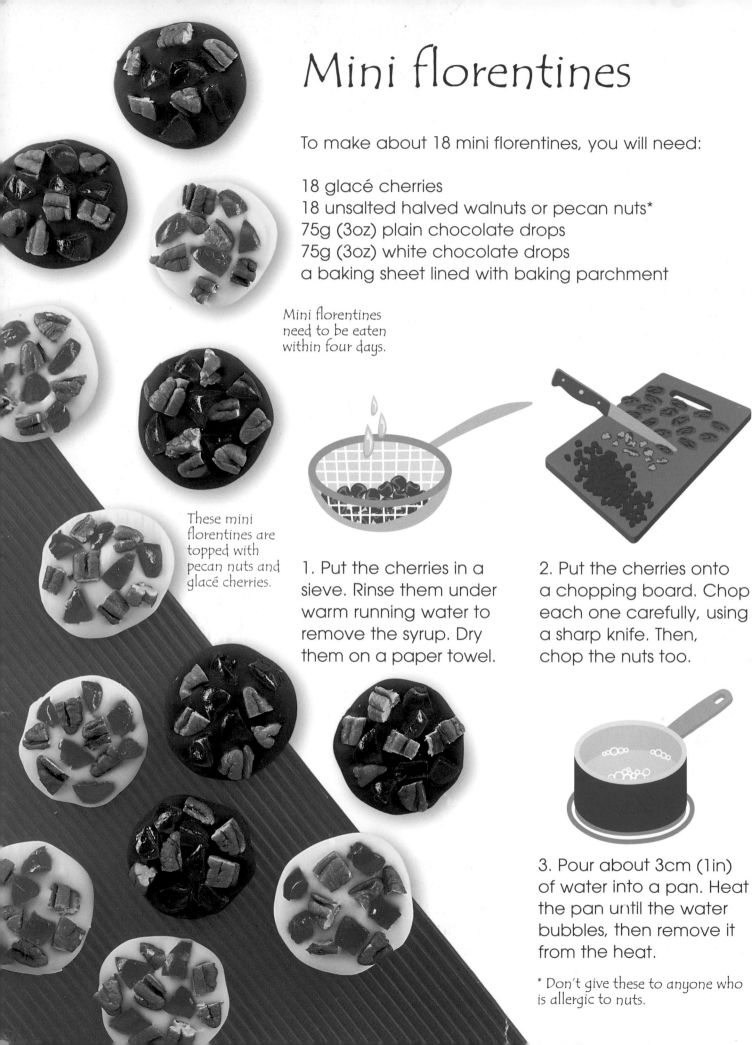

1. Put the cherries in a sieve. Rinse them under warm running water to remove the syrup. Dry them on a paper towel.

2. Put the cherries onto a chopping board. Chop each one carefully, using a sharp knife. Then, chop the nuts too.

3. Pour about 3cm (1in) of water into a pan. Heat the pan until the water bubbles, then remove it from the heat.

* Don't give these to anyone who is allergic to nuts.

4. Put the plain chocolate drops into a heatproof bowl. Wearing oven gloves, carefully put the bowl into the pan.

5. Stir the chocolate with a wooden spoon until it has melted. Using oven gloves, carefully lift the bowl out of the pan.

6. Spoon a teaspoon of melted chocolate onto the baking parchment. Make a neat circle, using the back of the spoon.

7. Gently press pieces of cherry and nut into the chocolate. Make more circles of chocolate and decorate them.

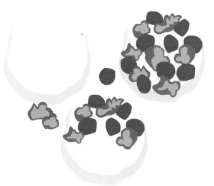

8. Then, melt the white chocolate drops. Make more circles with the chocolate and decorate them too.

9. Put the florentines in a fridge for half an hour. Then, carefully peel them off the paper. Keep them in an airtight container.

Chocolate swirls

To make about 25 chocolate swirls, you will need:

250g (9oz) icing sugar
half the white of a medium egg (3 teaspoons), mixed
 from dried egg white (mix as directed on the packet)
1 teaspoon of lemon juice
1 teaspoon of peppermint flavouring
1 tablespoon of cocoa powder
2 teaspoons boiling water
1 teaspoon of vanilla flavouring
a baking sheet covered in plastic foodwrap

Eat these within 10 days.

Pour the mixture into the hollow in the sugar.

1. Sift the icing sugar then put 100g (4oz) of it into a large bowl. Make a hollow in the middle with a spoon.

2. Mix half of the egg white with the lemon juice and peppermint in a small bowl. Pour the mixture into the sugar.

3. Stir the mixture with a blunt knife, then squeeze it with your fingers until it is smooth. Wrap it in plastic foodwrap.

If the mixture is a little dry, add a drop of water.

4. Sift the cocoa powder into a large bowl. Add the water and vanilla flavouring. Then, mix everything together well.

5. Add the rest of the egg white and stir it in. Add the rest of the icing sugar. Then, stir the mixture with a blunt knife.

6. Squeeze the mixture until it is smooth. Wrap it in foodwrap too. Put the two pieces in a fridge for 10 minutes.

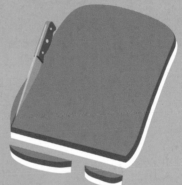

7. Sprinkle a little icing sugar onto a clean work surface and a rolling pin. The icing sugar stops the mixture from sticking.

8. Roll out the white mixture into a rectangle 20cm x 15cm (8in x 6in). Do the same with the chocolate mixture.

9. Put the chocolate rectangle on top of the white one. Then, trim the edges with a knife to make them straight.

Roll the rectangle from one of the long edges.

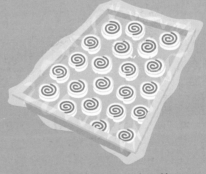

10. Tightly roll the rectangle into a sausage. Wrap it in foodwrap and put it in a fridge for about 10 minutes.

11. Using a sharp knife, carefully cut the sausage into slices which are about the thickness of your little finger.

12. Put the swirls onto the baking sheet. Leave them to harden overnight. Keep them in an airtight container.

Chocolate bugs

To make 10 bugs, you will need:

75g (3oz) plain chocolate drops
3 tablespoons golden syrup
75g (3oz) white chocolate drops

The bugs need
to be eaten
within a week.

Use a wooden spoon.

1. Pour about 3cm (1in) of water into a pan. Heat the pan until the water bubbles, then remove the pan from the heat.

2. Put the plain chocolate drops into a heatproof bowl. Using oven gloves, carefully put the bowl into the pan.

3. Stir the chocolate until it has melted. Wearing oven gloves, lift the bowl out of the pan. Leave it to cool for two minutes.

4. Stir in 1½ tablespoons of golden syrup until the mixture forms a thick paste which doesn't stick to the sides of the bowl.

5. Wrap the paste in plastic foodwrap. Then, melt the white chocolate and stir in the rest of the golden syrup, as before.

6. Wrap the white paste in plastic foodwrap. Chill both pieces of chocolate paste in a fridge for about an hour.

You could also decorate the bugs with stripes or wiggly lines.

7. Take both pieces of chocolate paste out of the fridge. Leave them for about 10 minutes, to soften a little.

8. Cut the plain chocolate paste into six pieces. Wrap one piece in foodwrap again and put it on one side.

9. Make the other five pieces into oval shapes. Do the same with the white chocolate paste, to make 10 ovals altogether.

Smooth the edges of the oval shapes.

Make a shallow mark with the knife.

The second mark makes the wings.

10. To make a bug's head, gently press in the back of a blunt knife, a third of the way down a chocolate shape.

11. Make a second mark. Unwrap the last pieces of paste. Roll small balls to make eyes and spots. Press them onto the bug.

12. Put the bugs onto a plate. Cover them with plastic foodwrap. Keep them in a fridge until you are ready to eat them.

Marshmallow crunch

To make about 50 squares, you will need:

25g (1oz) glacé cherries
75g (3oz) puffed rice cereal
100g (4oz) pink and white marshmallows
25g (1oz) butter
a shallow 18cm (7in) square cake tin
greaseproof paper

Marshmallow crunch needs
to be eaten within three days.

1. Put the tin onto a piece of greaseproof paper. Draw around it and cut out the square, just inside the line.

2. Use a paper towel to wipe some oil onto the sides and bottom of the tin. Press in the paper square and wipe it too.

3. Put the glacé cherries onto a chopping board. Carefully cut them into small pieces, using a sharp knife.

4. Put the puffed rice cereal and chopped cherries into a bowl. Mix them well with a wooden spoon.

5. Cut the marshmallows in half using a clean pair of scissors. Put the marshmallows and the butter into a large pan.

6. Gently heat the pan, stirring occasionally with a wooden spoon. Carry on until everything has just melted.

Use a wooden spoon.

Push the mixture into the corners and smooth it down.

7. Remove the pan from the heat. Add the cereal mixture to the pan and stir everything until it is mixed together.

8. Spoon the mixture into the tin, and put it in a fridge for two hours. Then, loosen the edges with a blunt knife.

9. Turn the crunch out onto a board. Remove the paper. Cut the crunch into squares. Keep it in an airtight container.

Peppermint creams

To make about 40 peppermint creams, you will need:

250g (9oz) icing sugar
half the white of a small egg (2½ teaspoons), mixed
   from dried egg white (mix as directed on the packet)
1 teaspoon of peppermint flavouring
2 teaspoons lemon juice
red and green food dye
small cutters
a baking sheet covered
   in plastic foodwrap

These sweets need to be eaten within two weeks.

1. Sift the icing sugar through a sieve into a large bowl. Make a hole in the middle of the sugar with a spoon.

2. Mix the egg white, peppermint flavouring and lemon juice in a small bowl. Pour the mixture into the sugar.

3. Use a blunt knife to stir the mixture. Squeeze it between your fingers until it is smooth. Then, cut it into two halves.

4. Put each half into a separate bowl. Add a few drops of red food dye to one bowl, and green dye to the other.

5. Mix in the red dye with your fingers. Add more icing sugar if the mixture is sticky. Mix the green dye into the other bowl.

6. Sprinkle a little icing sugar onto a clean work surface. Sprinkle some onto a rolling pin too, to stop the mixture sticking.

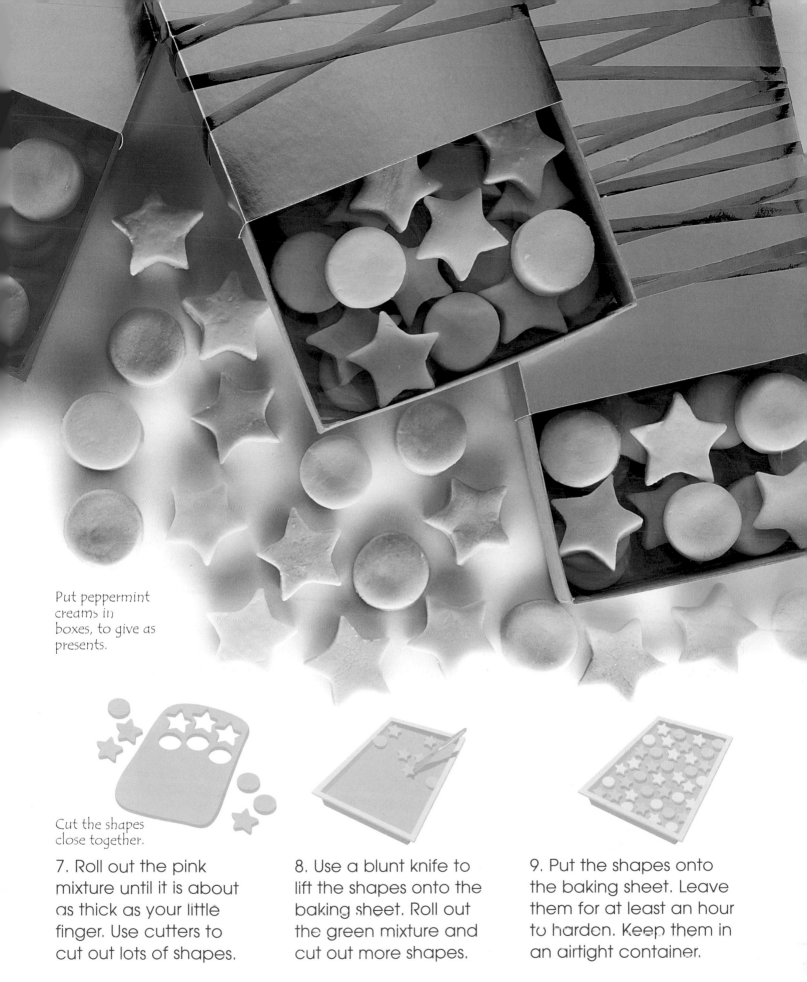

Put peppermint
creams in
boxes, to give as
presents.

Cut the shapes
close together.

7. Roll out the pink
mixture until it is about
as thick as your little
finger. Use cutters to
cut out lots of shapes.

8. Use a blunt knife to
lift the shapes onto the
baking sheet. Roll out
the green mixture and
cut out more shapes.

9. Put the shapes onto
the baking sheet. Leave
them for at least an hour
to harden. Keep them in
an airtight container.

21

Orange and lemon creams

To make about 24 orange and lemon creams, you will need:

350g (12oz) icing sugar
1 small orange
half the white of a small egg (2½ teaspoons), mixed from dried egg white (mix as directed on the packet)
red and yellow food dye
1 lemon
a baking sheet lined with greaseproof paper

These sweets need to be eaten within 10 days.

Sweetie bags filled with orange and lemon creams make great presents. Find out how to make them on page 30.

Use the small holes on a grater.

Use a lemon squeezer.

1. Sift half of the icing sugar into one bowl and half into another bowl. Then, grate about half of the skin of the orange.

2. Cut the orange in half and squeeze. Put the juice into a bowl. Then, put 1½ teaspoons of egg white into another bowl.

3. Add the grated orange, five teaspoons of juice, a drop of red food dye and two drops of yellow food dye. Mix everything well.

Squeeze the mixture until it is smooth.

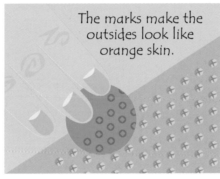

The marks make the outsides look like orange skin.

4. Add the mixture to one of the bowls of icing sugar. Stir it with a blunt knife, then squeeze it with your fingers.

5. Sprinkle icing sugar on a clean work surface. Make about 12 orange balls. Then, gently roll them over a fine grater.

6. Grate about half of the lemon's skin. Cut the lemon in half. Squeeze it and put five teaspoons of the juice into a bowl.

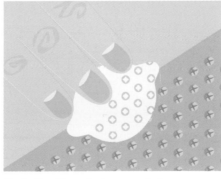

7. Add a few drops of yellow food dye, the grated lemon and 1½ teaspoons of egg white. Mix everything together.

8. Mix the juice mixture into the other bowl of icing sugar, as before. Make lemon shapes. Roll them over a fine grater.

9. Put the sweets onto the baking sheet. Leave them for a few hours to become firm. Keep them in an airtight container.

Magic marshmallow fudge

To make 36 pieces, you will need:

450g (1lb) icing sugar, preferably unrefined
100g (4oz) white marshmallows
2 tablespoons milk
100g (4oz) unsalted butter
half a teaspoon of vanilla essence
a shallow 18cm (7in) square cake tin
greaseproof paper

The fudge needs
to be eaten
within a week.

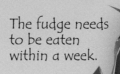

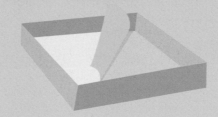

1. Put the tin onto a piece of greaseproof paper. Draw around it and cut out the square, just inside the line.

2. Use a paper towel to wipe some oil onto the sides and bottom of the tin. Press in the paper square and wipe it too.

3. Sift the icing sugar through a sieve into a large bowl. Make a small hollow in the middle of the icing sugar.

4. Using scissors, cut the marshmallows in half and put them into a small pan. Add the milk, butter and vanilla essence.

5. Gently heat the mixture. Stir it every now and then with a wooden spoon until everything has melted.

6. Pour the mixture into the hollow in the icing sugar. Beat everything together with a spoon until it is smooth.

Smooth the fudge
with the back of
a spoon.

7. Put the fudge into the
tin and push it into the
corners. Use a spoon to
make the top of the
fudge as flat as you can.

Find out how to wrap pieces
of fudge like this on page 31.

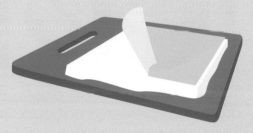

8. When the fudge is
cool, put the tin in a
fridge for about three
hours, or until the
fudge is firm.

9. Use a blunt knife to
loosen the edges of the
fudge, then turn it out
onto a chopping board.
Remove the paper.

10. Cut the fudge into
36 pieces. Then, put it
in a fridge for an hour
to harden. Keep it in an
airtight container.

Chocolate fudge

To make about 36 squares, you will need:

75g (3oz) full-fat cream cheese
350g (12oz) icing sugar
1 level tablespoon of cocoa powder
75g (3oz) plain chocolate drops
40g (1½oz) butter
greaseproof paper
a shallow 15cm (6in) square cake tin

The fudge needs to be eaten within a week.

Find out how to make pointed gift bags on page 30.

Use a pencil to draw around the tin.

1. Put the tin onto a sheet of greaseproof paper. Draw around it and cut out the square, just inside the line.

2. Use a paper towel to wipe some oil onto the sides and bottom of the tin. Press in the paper square and wipe it too.

3. Put the cream cheese into a bowl. Sift the icing sugar and cocoa through a sieve into the bowl too. Mix them together well.

4. Melt the chocolate and butter as in steps 1-3 on page 9. Stir in a tablespoon of the cream cheese mixture.

5. Then, pour the chocolate into the cheese mixture. Beat them together with a spoon until they are creamy.

6. Spoon the mixture into the tin, and push it into the corners. You may need to use your fingers to do this.

7. Smooth the top of the fudge with the back of a spoon. Put the tin in a fridge for two hours, or until the fudge is firm.

8. Use a blunt knife to loosen the edges of the fudge, then turn it out onto a chopping board. Remove the paper.

9. Cut the fudge into 36 squares. Put it in a fridge for two hours, to harden. Keep it in the fridge in an airtight container.

Wrapping ideas

Sweetie bags

1. Cut a square of thin cellophane. Then, lay five or six sweets or chocolates in the middle of the square.

2. Gather up the edges of the square around the sweets. Then, pull the edges together above the sweets, like this.

3. Cut a piece of parcel ribbon about 20cm (8in) long. Tie the ribbon tightly around the bag, above the sweets.

Pointed bags

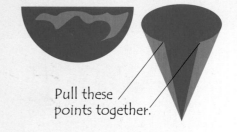

The white line shows you where to cut.

Pull these points together.

1. Cut a square of cellophane with sides 40cm (16in) long. Fold it in half, and then in half again.

2. Hold the corner where the folds join. Cut a quarter-circle, like this. Open out the cellophane shape. It is now a circle.

3. Cut the circle in half. Take one of the halves. Then, pull its two points towards each other until they meet.

4. Slide one of the points behind the other, to make a cone. Secure the cone with some [pie]ces of sticky tape.

5. Half-fill the cone with sweets. Cut a piece of parcel ribbon 20cm (8in) long. Tie it around the cone, above the sweets.

Line a gift box with cellophane, then fill it with layers of sweets.

Wrapped sweets

Find out how to make sparkling gift tags on page 32.

1. Cut a square of thin cellophane that is bigger than the sweet. Put the sweet in the middle of the square.

2. Wrap the sweet in the piece of cellophane and tape it. Tie pieces of parcel ribbon around each end of the sweet.

Use a tiny piece of tape.

Sparkling gift tags

Ask someone to help you cut the potato.

1. Carefully cut a potato in half. Press the sharp edge of a star-shaped cookie cutter into the cut side of the potato.

2. Press the edge of the star cutter into some PVA glue. Press the cutter onto a piece of thin cardboard.

3. Before the glue dries, sprinkle it with lots of glitter. Shake off any extra glitter onto some scrap paper.

4. Cut around the star, a little way away from the glitter. Tape a piece of parcel ribbon to the back of the tag.